S0-AWJ-597

A Treasury
of
Abbey Favorites

ISBN: 0-87029-197-1
© 1986 St. Meinrad Archabbey
St. Meinrad, Indiana 47577

A Treasury

OF

ABBEY FAVORITES

*Favorite reflections . . .
for you,
for every day.*

CONTENTS

F A I T H

FOOTPRINTS IN THE SAND

One night I had a dream. I was walking along the beach with the Lord, and across the skies flashed scenes from my life. In each scene I noticed two sets of footprints in the sand. One was mine, and one was the Lord's. When the last scene of my life appeared before me, I looked back at the footprints in the sand, and, to my surprise, I noticed that many times along the path of my life there was only one set of footprints. And I noticed that it was at the lowest and saddest times in my life. I asked the Lord about it: "Lord, you said that once I decided to follow you, you would walk with me all the way. But I notice that during the most troublesome times in my life there is only one set of footprints. I don't understand why you left my side when I needed you most." The Lord said: "My precious child, I never left you during your time of trial. Where you see only one set of footprints, I was carrying you."

THE DIFFERENCE

I got up early one morning
and rushed right into the day:
  I had so much to accomplish
  that I didn't have time to pray.
Problems just tumbled about me,
and heavier came each task.
  "Why doesn't God help me?"
  I wondered.
  He answered, "You didn't ask."
I wanted to see joy and beauty,
but the day toiled on, gray and bleak:
  I wondered why
  God didn't show me.
  He said, "But you didn't seek."
I tried to come into God's presence:
I used all my keys at the lock.
  God gently and lovingly chided,
  "My child, you didn't knock."
I woke up early this morning
and paused before entering the day;
  I had so much to accomplish
  that I had to take time to pray.

GOD wrote His promise to us with love
and signed it with a rainbow.

IF GOD can paint a rainbow
from the weeping skies above,
just think what He can do
with human teardrops and His love.

BROKEN DREAMS

As children bring
   their broken toys
   with tears for us
   to mend,
I brought my
   broken dreams to God
   because He was
   my friend.

But then instead
   of leaving Him
   in peace to work alone,
I hung around and
   tried to help
   with ways
   that were my own.

At last I snatched them
   back and cried,
"How can You be so slow"—
"My child," He said,
   "What could I do?
   You never did let go."

IN HIS HANDS . . .

The hands that made the world
and gave the sun and moon their light
are the tiny hands of a baby born
one cold December night : . .
The hands that stilled the wind
and turned the fury of the sea
are the calloused hands of a carpenter
Who lived in poverty . . .
The hands that held the power
to break the binding chains of sin
are the gentle hands that washed the feet
of tired and dusty men . . .
The hands that cleansed the leper,
healed the blind, and raised the dead
are the praying hands of One Who cried,
"Not my will, but Thine instead . . ."
The hands that shaped the universe
and flung the stars in space
are the nail-pierced hands of a dying man
who suffered in our place . . .
The hands of our Creator,
Lord and King of Heaven above
are the Savior's hands,
forever reaching out to us with love . . .

B.J. Hoff

DON'T QUIT

When things go wrong
as they sometimes will,
When the road you're trudging
seems all uphill,
When the funds are low,
and the debts are high,
And you want to smile,
but you have to sigh,
When care is pressing you down a bit—
Rest if you must, but don't you quit.

Success is failure turned inside out,
The silver tint of the clouds of doubt,
And you never can tell how close you are,
It may be near when it seems afar,
So, stick to the fight
when you're hardest hit—
It's when things go wrong
that you mustn't quit.

LOVE

&

FRIENDSHIP

A FRIEND is one to whom one may pour
out all the contents of one's heart,
chaff and grain together, knowing that
the gentlest of hands will take and sift it,
keep what is worth keeping and with the
breath of kindness, blow the rest away.

Arabian Proverb

WHEN YOU'RE LONELY

When you're lonely
  I wish you love.
When you're down
  I wish you joy.
When you're troubled
  I wish you peace.
When things are complicated
  I wish you simple beauty.
When things are chaotic
  I wish you inner silence.
When things look empty
  I wish you hope.

FRIENDSHIP doubles our joy
and divides our grief.

IT DOESN'T matter where you go,
what you do or how much you have,
it's who you have beside you.

LOVE . . .

is patient, love is kind.
Love is not jealous,
it does not put on airs,
it is not snobbish.
Love is never rude,
it is not self-seeking,
it is not prone to anger;
neither does it brood over injuries.
Love does not rejoice in what is wrong,
but rejoices with the truth.
There is no limit to love's forbearance,
its truth, its hope, its power to endure.

1 Corinthians 13:4-7

THE WAY IS LONG

The way is long—
  Let us go together
The way is difficult—
  Let us help each other
The way is joyful—
  Let us share it
The way is ours alone—
  Let us go in love
The way opens before us—
  Let us begin

GOD IS LOVE—
Anyone who abides in love,
abides in God.

1 John 4:16

FAMILY

As FOR ME and my house
we will serve the Lord.

Joshua 24:15

THESE THINGS a mother gives us
from the treasury of her heart:
the gentle gift of tenderness . . .
a daily gift of happiness . . .
her lifetime gift of love for us . . .

ANYONE can be a father,
but it takes someone special
to be a daddy.

CHILDREN LEARN WHAT THEY LIVE

If children live with criticism,
    they learn to condemn.
If children live with hostility,
    they learn to fight.
If children live with ridicule,
    they learn to be shy.
If children live with shame,
    they learn to feel guilty.
If children live with tolerance,
    they learn to be patient.
If children live with encouragement,
    they learn confidence.
If children live with praise,
    they learn to appreciate.
If children live with fairness,
    they learn justice.
If children live with security,
    they learn to have faith.
If children live with approval,
    they learn to like themselves.
If children live with
    acceptance and friendship,
    they learn to find love in the world.

RECIPE FOR A HAPPY HOME

Combine happy hearts
Melt hearts into one
Add a lot of love
Mix well with respect
Add gentleness, laughter, joy,
faith, hope and self-control
Pour in much understanding
Don't forget the patience
Blend in listening ears
Allow to grow and share
Sprinkle with smiles,
hugs, and kisses
Bake for a lifetime
YIELD: ONE HAPPY HOME

PRAYERS FOR ALL SEASONS

LORD, make me
   an instrument of Your peace.

Where there is hatred,
   let me sow love.
Where there is injury,
   pardon.
Where there is doubt,
   faith.
Where there is despair,
   hope.
Where there is darkness,
   light.
Where there is sadness,
   joy.

Prayer of St. Francis

PRAYER FOR AMERICA

We are America . . .
The heart of a world
seeking freedom and peace,
We are the east and the west,
the north and the south—
one people embracing many.
We are a legacy of courage
with a destiny for greatness.
We are history and prophecy,
liberty and home, refuge and vision.

So we lift up our light as a beacon of hope,
with this prayer to our God and Creator:
Make us a people who care and who comfort,
Let us reach out a welcoming hand
to the homeless, the helpless,
the hurting, the hungry.
Let us fulfill God's great plan for our land.
Let our gift to the nations be love.

B.J. Hoff

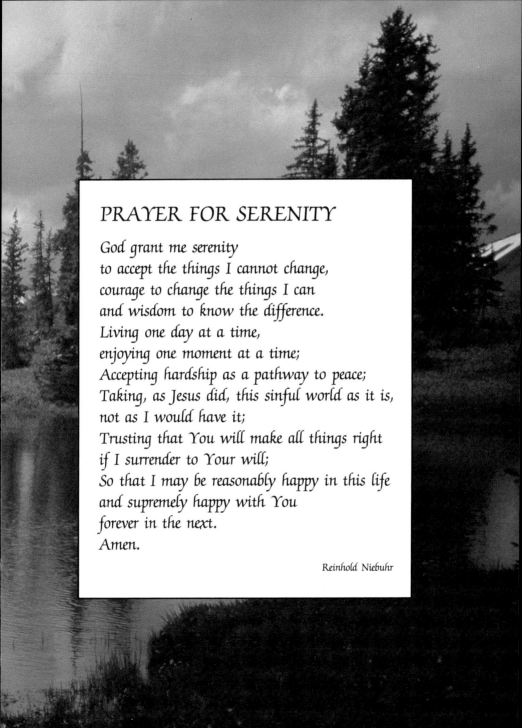

PRAYER FOR SERENITY

God grant me serenity
to accept the things I cannot change,
courage to change the things I can
and wisdom to know the difference.
Living one day at a time,
enjoying one moment at a time;
Accepting hardship as a pathway to peace;
Taking, as Jesus did, this sinful world as it is,
not as I would have it;
Trusting that You will make all things right
if I surrender to Your will;
So that I may be reasonably happy in this life
and supremely happy with You
forever in the next.
Amen.

Reinhold Niebuhr

"I AM with you always,
even to the end of the world."

Matthew 28:20

LORD, today, and in each moment of my life,
    open my mind and heart to life
    so that I am not dead as I live.
Fill me with the Presence of God;
    let me live in His Kingdom;
    fill me even to overflowing
    so that some spills out on the world.

C.J. Brown

THE LORD bless you and keep you:

The Lord make His face to shine upon you,
    and be gracious to you:
The Lord lift up His countenance upon you,
    and give you peace.

Numbers 6:24-26

ACKNOWLEDGEMENTS

PHOTO CREDITS: Cover photograph courtesy of Carl K. Kendrick, Jr.; Page 3 photograph courtesy of St. Meinrad Archabbey; Page 44-45 photograph courtesy of Sr. Mary Jonathan Schultz; Edward & Chris Kumler, Pages 4-5, 8-9, 12-13, 14-15, 18-19, 22-23, 26-27, 28-29, 30-31, 32-33, 34-35, 38-39, 40-41; L.M. Falkenberry/FPG, Pages 10-11; Dennis Hallinan/FPG, Pages 20-21, 24-25; Gay Bumgarner, 36-37; Kathi Bartley, Pages 6-7, 16-17; Tim Weyer, 42-43

TEXT CREDITS: B.J. Hoff, Pages 14, 40; C.J. Brown, Page 45; All rights reserved by Abbey Press.

BOOK DESIGN: Sharon Hueston-Lueken